CONTENTS

MARRIAGE AND THE BLESSING OF A MARRIAGE

INTRODUCTION

A marriage ceremony is a formal occasion when a solemn, legal contract is made between a man and a woman. In a Christian context, it is also an act of worship in which marriage is celebrated as a gift of God and the joy of the couple is shared and their commitment to each other is witnessed by family and friends. *The Marriage Service*'s themes of love, hope, faithfulness, sacrifice and trust are at the heart of the Christian gospel.

The Blessing of a Marriage Previously Solemnized also gives expression to these themes. It is intended for those whose marriage was solemnized in a civil ceremony and who later desire the blessing of that marriage in an act of Christian worship.

THE MARRIAGE SERVICE

NOTES

1 At the time of publication, it is required by law in England and Wales that the words of declaration at no. 5 and the words of contract at no. 13 (or the permitted alternative forms, set out in the Appendix on page 384) should be said in the presence of the Authorized Person (or the Registrar) and two witnesses. The full names of the parties should be used.

2 When this service is used in Scotland, the Channel Islands, the Isle of Man, Northern Ireland, the Republic of Ireland, or any other jurisdiction whose marriage legislation is different from that of England and Wales, the minister should ensure that the service complies with the legal requirements of that jurisdiction. Appropriate substitutions should be made at nos. 5 and 13 if necessary.

THE PREPARATION

1 The people stand as the bridal or marriage party enters the church. The persons to be married stand together before the minister, the woman on the left of the man.

The minister may welcome the congregation.

The minister says:

> We meet together in the presence of God
> to witness the marriage of *A* and *C*,
> to ask God's blessing upon them,
> to support them with our prayers
> and to share their joy.

2 Hymn

3 The people remain standing. The minister says:

> Let us pray.
>
> Gracious God, your generous love surrounds us,
> and everything we enjoy comes from you.
> We confess our ingratitude for your goodness
> and our selfishness in using your gifts.
> Forgive and renew us,
> and fill us with your Spirit
> that in true thankfulness
> we may bear witness to your love;
> through Jesus Christ our Lord. **Amen.**

4 The minister says:

> *A* and *C*, with your families and friends,
> we thank God on this day
> for the gift of marriage.
>
> It is the will of God that, in marriage,
> husband and wife should experience
> a life-long unity of heart, body and mind;
> comfort and companionship;
> enrichment and encouragement;
> tenderness and trust.
>
> It is the will of God that marriage
> should be honoured as a way of life,
> in which we may know the security of love and care,
> and grow towards maturity.
> Through such marriage,
> children may be nurtured,
> family life strengthened,
> and human society enriched.
>
> No one should enter into this lightly or selfishly,
> for marriage involves the giving
> of a man and a woman
> wholeheartedly to each other.
> Christ in his self-giving comes to our help,
> for he loves us and gave himself for us.
>
> *A* and *C*, you are now to share this way of life
> which God has created
> and, in Christ, has blessed.
> Today we pray that the Holy Spirit
> will guide and strengthen you
> that you may fulfil God's purposes
> for the rest of your lives.

5 The Legal Declarations

The minister says to the people:

> *A* and *C* are now to make the declarations which the law requires.

The minister says to the man:

> Are you, *AB*, free lawfully to marry *CD*?

The man answers: I am.

The minister says to the woman:

> Are you, *CD*, free lawfully to marry *AB*?

The woman answers: I am.

6 The minister says to the man and the woman:

> You have made the declarations required by law. I ask you now to affirm, in the presence of us all, your intention to marry each other.

The minister says to the man:

> *A*, are you willing to give yourself in marriage to *C*?

The man answers: I am.

The minister says to the man:

> Will you love her, comfort and honour her, be her companion through all the joys and sorrows of life, and be faithful to her as long as you both shall live?

The man answers: With God's help, I will.

The minister says to the woman:

> *C*, are you willing to give yourself in marriage to *A*?

The woman answers: I am.

The minister says to the woman:

Will you love him, comfort and honour him, be his companion through all the joys and sorrows of life, and be faithful to him as long as you both shall live?

The woman answers: **With God's help, I will.**

THE MINISTRY OF THE WORD

The whole of the Ministry of the Word may occur here or at no. 18, or the scripture readings may be read here and the sermon may be preached at no. 18.

7 All sit. At least one passage of scripture is read. If Holy Communion is to be celebrated, a passage from the Gospels always concludes the readings.

Many waters cannot quench love, neither can floods drown it. If one offered for love all the wealth of one's house, it would be utterly scorned.

Song of Solomon 8:7

Love is patient; love is kind; love is not envious or boastful or arrogant or rude. It does not insist on its own way; it is not irritable or resentful; it does not rejoice in wrongdoing, but rejoices in the truth. It bears all things, believes all things, hopes all things, endures all things. Love never ends.

And now faith, hope, and love abide, these three; and the greatest of these is love.

1 Corinthians 13:4-8*a*, 13

For this reason I bow my knees before the Father, from whom every family in heaven and on earth takes its name. I pray that, according to the riches of his glory, he may grant that you may be strengthened in your inner being with power through his Spirit, and that Christ may dwell in your hearts through faith, as you are being rooted and grounded in love.
I pray that you may have the power to comprehend, with all the saints, what is the breadth and length and height and depth, and to know the love of Christ that surpasses knowledge, so that you may be filled with all the fullness of God.

Ephesians 3:14-19

As God's chosen ones, holy and beloved, clothe yourselves with compassion, kindness, humility, meekness, and patience. Bear with one another and, if anyone has a complaint against another, forgive each other; just as the Lord has forgiven you, so you also must forgive. Above all, clothe yourselves with love, which binds everything together in perfect harmony. And let the peace of Christ rule in your hearts, to which indeed you were called in the one body. And be thankful. Let the word of Christ dwell in you richly; teach and admonish one another in all wisdom; and with gratitude in your hearts sing psalms, hymns and spiritual songs to God. And whatever you do, in word or deed, do everything in the name of the Lord Jesus, giving thanks to God the Father through him.

Colossians 3:12-17

Jesus said: 'From the beginning of creation, "God made them male and female." "For this reason a man shall leave his father and mother and be joined to his wife, and the two shall become one flesh." So they are no longer two, but one flesh. Therefore what God has joined together, let no one separate.'

Mark 10:6-9

Jesus said: 'As the Father has loved me, so I have loved you; abide in my love. If you keep my commandments, you will abide in my love, just as I have kept my Father's commandments and abide in his love. I have said these things to you so that my joy may be in you, and that your joy may be complete. This is my commandment, that you love one another as I have loved you.'

John 15:9-12

Additional scripture readings are listed on page 398.

8 Sermon

9 Hymn

THE MARRIAGE

10 All stand. The minister may say to the people:

I ask you, the families and friends of *A* and *C*:

Will you do all in your power to support and encourage them in their marriage?

The people answer:

With God's help, we will.

11 If the woman has a relative or friend presenting her for marriage, the minister says:

Who presents *C* to be married to *A*?

The woman's relative or friend answers: **I do.**

If the man has a relative or friend presenting him for marriage, the minister says:

Who presents *A* to be married to *C*?

The man's relative or friend answers: **I do.**

12 The minister says:

> Gracious God,
> as you have brought *A* and *C* together in love and trust,
> enable them through the power of your Holy Spirit
> to make and keep their vows;
> through Jesus Christ our Lord. **Amen.**

13 The Vows

The man takes the woman's right hand in his and says to her:

> **I, *AB*, take you, *CD*, to be my wedded wife,**
> for better, for worse,
> for richer, for poorer,
> in sickness and in health,
> to love and to cherish,
> from this day forward,
> until we are parted by death;
> and this is my solemn vow.

They loose hands.

The woman takes the man's right hand in hers and says to him:

> **I, *CD*, take you, *AB*, to be my wedded husband,**
> for better, for worse,
> for richer, for poorer,
> in sickness and in health,
> to love and to cherish,
> from this day forward,
> until we are parted by death;
> and this is my solemn vow.

They loose hands.

14 The Giving of the Ring(s)

IF TWO RINGS ARE BEING GIVEN	IF ONLY ONE RING IS BEING GIVEN

The minister receives the rings on the book, and says:

The minister receives the ring on the book, and says:

Eternal God,
bless these rings
that they may be
symbols of the love and
    trust
between *A* and *C*. **Amen.**

Eternal God,
bless this ring,
that it may be
a symbol of the love and
    trust
between *A* and *C*. **Amen.**

EITHER

EITHER

The man places a ring on the woman's ring finger, and says:

The man places the ring on the woman's ring finger, and says:

I give you this ring
as a sign of our marriage.
With my body I honour
    you,
all that I am I give to you,
and all that I have
I share with you,
within the love of God,
Father, Son and Holy
    Spirit.

I give you this ring
as a sign of our marriage.
With my body I honour
    you,
all that I am I give to you,
and all that I have
I share with you,
within the love of God,
Father, Son and Holy
    Spirit.

The woman places a ring on the man's ring finger, and says:

The woman says:

I give you this ring
as a sign of our marriage.
With my body I honour
    you,
all that I am I give to you,
and all that I have
I share with you,
within the love of God,
Father, Son and Holy
    Spirit.

I receive this ring
as a sign of our marriage.
With my body I honour
    you,
all that I am I give to you,
and all that I have
I share with you,
within the love of God,
Father, Son and Holy
    Spirit.

OR

After the rings have been given and received, the man and the woman say together:

**With these rings
we pledge ourselves
to each other,
in the Name of the Father,
and of the Son,
and of the Holy Spirit.**

OR

After the ring has been given and received, the man and the woman say together:

**With this ring
we pledge ourselves
to each other,
in the Name of the Father,
and of the Son,
and of the Holy Spirit.**

15   The minister joins the right hands of the man and the woman. The minister may wrap her/his stole around, and/or place her/his hand on their joined hands.

The minister says to the man and the woman:

**A and C, God so join you together
that none shall ever part you.**

The minister says to the people:

**Before God and in the presence of us all,
A and C have exchanged vows,
joined their hands,
and given and received *rings/a ring*,
binding themselves to each other
in the covenant of marriage.
I therefore proclaim
that they are now husband and wife.**

16   A hymn may be sung here or after no. 17.

17 The people remain standing. The husband and wife may kneel and the minister may lay hands upon their heads.

The minister says:

> *A* and *C,*
> the blessing of God the Father,
> God the Son, and God the Holy Spirit,
> be upon you and remain with you always.
> May God be your protection and your wisdom,
> your guide and your peace,
> your joy, your comfort, and your eternal rest. **Amen.**

18 The whole of the Ministry of the Word follows, if it has not occurred earlier. If the sermon has been deferred, it is preached here.

THE PRAYERS

19 These or some other prayers of intercession:

> Let us pray.
>
> God of grace, source of all love,
> we pray for *A* and *C*
> that they may live together in love and faithfulness
> to the end of their lives.
>
> Lord of life,
> **hear us in your love.**
>
> Enrich their friendship,
> that each may be for the other
> a companion in joy and a comforter in sorrow.
>
> Lord of life,
> **hear us in your love.**
>
> Help *A* and *C* to be patient, gentle and forgiving,
> that their marriage may reflect Christ's love for all people.
>
> Lord of life,
> **hear us in your love.**

Enable them to make their home
a place of welcome and friendship,
that their life together
may be a source of strength to others.

Lord of life,
hear us in your love.

Other intercessions may be included.

May we, who have witnessed these vows today,
be signs of your love in the world;
through Jesus Christ our Lord. **Amen.**

20 The Lord's Prayer

EITHER

We say together the prayer
that Jesus gave us:

**Our Father in heaven,
hallowed be your Name,
your kingdom come,
your will be done,
on earth as in heaven.
Give us today our daily
   bread.
Forgive us our sins
as we forgive those who
   sin against us.
Save us from the time of
   trial
and deliver us from evil.
For the kingdom, the
   power and the glory
   are yours,
now and for ever. Amen.**

OR

As our Saviour taught his
disciples, we pray:

**Our Father, who art in
   heaven,
hallowed be thy Name;
thy kingdom come;
thy will be done;
on earth as it is in heaven.
Give us this day our
   daily bread.
And forgive us our
   trespasses,
as we forgive those who
   trespass against us.
And lead us not into
   temptation;
but deliver us from evil.
For thine is the kingdom,
   the power, and the
   glory,
for ever and ever. Amen.**

21 If Holy Communion is to be celebrated, the service continues
from no. 25.

If Holy Communion is not celebrated, the service continues as follows:

22 All stand.

The minister says this prayer, or gives thanks in her/his own words:

> Praise God,
> who is the source of joy and celebration,
> pleasure and delight, love and friendship.
>
> Praise God,
> who, in the life and victory of Jesus Christ,
> reveals to us the glory of self-giving love.
>
> Praise God,
> who sends the Holy Spirit to be our helper
> and to guide us into the way of perfect love.
>
> **Praise God, Father, Son, and Holy Spirit. Amen.**

23 Hymn

24 The minister says to all present:

> God the Father, God the Son,
> and God the Holy Spirit,
> make *you/us* strong in faith
> and guide *you/us* in truth and love.

EITHER

> The Lord bless you
>   and keep you;
> the Lord make his face to
>   shine on you
> and be gracious to you;
> the Lord look on you with
>   kindness
> and give you peace. **Amen.**

OR

> May God be gracious to us
>   and bless us,
> and make his face to shine
>   upon us. **Amen.**

HOLY COMMUNION

25 The Peace

All stand.

> The peace of the Lord be always with you.
> **And also with you.**

The people may greet one another in the name of Christ.

THE PREPARATION OF THE GIFTS

26 Bread and wine are brought to the table by the husband and wife or other members of the congregation (or if already on the table are uncovered). The presiding minister takes the bread and wine and prepares them for use.

THE THANKSGIVING

27 All stand.

The presiding minister leads the great prayer of thanksgiving:

> The Lord be with you.
> **And also with you.**
>
> Lift up your hearts.
> **We lift them to the Lord.**
>
> Let us give thanks to the Lord our God.
> **It is right to give our thanks and praise.**
>
> We praise you, gracious God,
> creator and sustainer of all things.
>
> From the beginning
> you made man and woman
> for yourself and for each other,
> and you call us to reflect your faithfulness
> in lives of love and service.

You gave yourself to us in your Son, Jesus Christ,
the Lord of heaven and earth,
and entrusted him to the care of a human family.
In his life, death and resurrection,
you revealed the power of self-giving love,
rescued us from sin and selfishness,
and made us a new family through your grace.

You give yourself to us today,
and by your Holy Spirit
you promise to be with us always
as our companion and our guide.

And so, with all your people on earth and in heaven,
we give you thanks and praise:

Holy, holy, holy Lord,
God of power and might,
heaven and earth are full of your glory.
Hosanna in the highest.
Blessèd is he who comes in the name of the Lord.
Hosanna in the highest.

Holy God, we praise you
that on the night in which he was betrayed
our Saviour Christ took bread
and gave you thanks.
He broke it, and gave it to his disciples, saying,
'Take, eat. This is my body, given for you.
Do this in remembrance of me.'

After supper, he took the cup of wine,
gave thanks, and gave it to them, saying,
'Drink this, all of you.
This is my blood of the new covenant,
poured out for all people for the forgiveness of sins.
Do this in remembrance of me.'

And so, gracious God, we remember and celebrate
all that Christ has done for us.
We offer ourselves to you in humble thanksgiving.

Send your Holy Spirit
that these gifts of bread and wine
may be for us the body and blood of Christ.
Together with all your people,
may we have life in all its fullness,
live in the power of love,
and fill creation with a song of endless praise.

**Through Christ, with Christ, and in Christ,
in the unity of the Holy Spirit,
all glory is yours, God most holy,
now and for ever. Amen.**

THE BREAKING OF THE BREAD

28 The presiding minister breaks the bread in the sight of the
people in silence, or saying:

The bread we break is a sharing in the body of Christ.

The presiding minister may lift the cup in silence, or saying:

The cup we bless is a sharing in the blood of Christ.

29 Silence, all seated or kneeling

THE SHARING OF THE BREAD AND WINE

30 The presiding minister receives, then, beginning with the
husband and wife and their families, the people, according to
local custom.

31 Words such as the following are said during the distribution:

The body of Christ. **Amen.**

The blood of Christ. **Amen.**

32 During the distribution there may be appropriate music.

33 The elements that remain are covered with a white cloth.

PRAYERS AND DISMISSAL

34 Let us pray.

**We thank you, Lord,
that you have fed us in this sacrament,
united us with Christ,
and given us a foretaste of the heavenly banquet
prepared for all people. Amen.**

35 Hymn

36 The presiding minister says to all present:

God the Father, God the Son,
and God the Holy Spirit,
make *you/us* strong in faith
and guide *you/us* in truth and love.

EITHER

The Lord bless you
    and keep you;
the Lord make his face to
    shine on you
and be gracious to you;
the Lord look on you with
    kindness
and give you peace. **Amen.**

OR

May God be gracious to us
    and bless us,
and make his face to shine
    upon us. **Amen.**

APPENDIX

1 As an alternative to the questions and answers in no. 5, the persons contracting the marriage may make the declaration required by law by saying:

EITHER

A I do solemnly declare
that I know not
of any lawful impediment
why I, *AB/CD,**
may not be joined in matrimony
to *CD/AB.**

OR

B I declare that I know of no legal reason why I,
AB/CD, * **may not be joined in marriage to** *CD/AB.**

2 As an alternative to the words of contract set out in no. 13,

EITHER

A the persons to be married may say:

I call upon these persons here present
to witness that I, *AB/CD,**
do take thee, *CD/AB,* *
to be my lawful wedded *wife/husband,*
for better, for worse,
for richer, for poorer,
in sickness and in health,
to love and to cherish,
from this day forward,
until we are parted by death;
and this is my solemn vow.

OR

B the persons to be married may say to each other:

I, *AB/CD,** **take thee,** *CD/AB,**
to be my wedded *wife/husband,*
for better, for worse,
for richer, for poorer,
in sickness and in health,
to love and to cherish,
from this day forward,
until we are parted by death;
and this is my solemn vow.

(* The full names of the parties must be used.)

THE BLESSING OF A MARRIAGE
PREVIOUSLY SOLEMNIZED

NOTES

1 This form of service must not be used for the solemnization of a marriage.

2 This form of service is not suitable for those who wish to reaffirm or renew marriage vows.

3 This service should normally be conducted by the minister with pastoral charge of the church in which it takes place. It can be used either as a private ceremony or with a congregation of family and friends.

THE PREPARATION

1 The persons whose marriage is to be blessed stand together before the minister, the wife on the left of her husband.

The minister may welcome the congregation.

The minister says:

We meet together in the presence of God
to join with A and C,
in asking God's blessing upon their marriage.

2 Hymn

3 The minister says:

A and C, with your families and friends,
we thank God on this day
for the gift of marriage.

It is the will of God that, in marriage,
husband and wife should experience
a life-long unity of heart, body and mind;
comfort and companionship;
enrichment and encouragement;
tenderness and trust.

It is the will of God that marriage
should be honoured as a way of life,
in which we may know the security of love and care,
and grow towards maturity.
Through such marriage,
children may be nurtured,
family life strengthened,
and human society enriched.

No one should enter into this lightly or selfishly,
for marriage involves the giving
of a man and a woman
wholeheartedly to each other.
Christ in his self-giving comes to our help,
for he loves us and gave himself for us.

A and *C*,
you have already entered this way of life
which God has created
and, in Christ, has blessed.
Today we pray that the Holy Spirit
will guide and strengthen you
that you may fulfil God's purposes
for the rest of your lives.

THE MINISTRY OF THE WORD

The whole of the Ministry of the Word may occur here or at no. 13, or the scripture readings may be read here and the sermon may be preached at no. 13.

4 All sit. At least one passage of scripture is read. If Holy Communion is to be celebrated, a passage from the Gospels always concludes the readings.

Many waters cannot quench love, neither can floods drown it. If one offered for love all the wealth of one's house, it would be utterly scorned.

Song of Solomon 8:7

Love is patient; love is kind; love is not envious or boastful or arrogant or rude. It does not insist on its own way; it is not irritable or resentful; it does not rejoice in wrongdoing, but rejoices in the truth. It bears all things, believes all things, hopes all things, endures all things. Love never ends.

And now faith, hope, and love abide, these three; and the greatest of these is love.

1 Corinthians 13:4-8*a*, 13

For this reason I bow my knees before the Father, from whom every family in heaven and on earth takes its name. I pray that, according to the riches of his glory, he may grant that you may be strengthened in your inner being with power through his Spirit, and that Christ may dwell in your hearts through faith, as you are being rooted and grounded in love.
I pray that you may have the power to comprehend, with all the saints, what is the breadth and length and height and depth, and to know the love of Christ that surpasses knowledge, so that you may be filled with all the fullness of God.

Ephesians 3:14-19

As God's chosen ones, holy and beloved, clothe yourselves with compassion, kindness, humility, meekness, and patience. Bear with one another and, if anyone has a complaint against another, forgive each other; just as the Lord has forgiven you, so you also must forgive. Above all, clothe yourselves with love, which binds everything together in perfect harmony. And let the peace of Christ rule in your hearts, to which indeed you were called in the one body. And be thankful. Let the word of Christ dwell in you richly; teach and admonish one another in all wisdom; and with gratitude in your hearts sing psalms, hymns and spiritual songs to God. And whatever you do, in word or deed, do everything in the name of the Lord Jesus, giving thanks to God the Father through him.

Colossians 3:12-17

Jesus said: 'From the beginning of creation, "God made them male and female." "For this reason a man shall leave his father and mother and be joined to his wife, and the two shall become one flesh." So they are no longer two, but one flesh. Therefore what God has joined together, let no one separate.'

Mark 10:6-9

Jesus said: 'As the Father has loved me, so I have loved you; abide in my love. If you keep my commandments, you will abide in my love, just as I have kept my Father's commandments and abide in his love. I have said these things to you so that my joy may be in you, and that your joy may be complete. This is my commandment, that you love one another as I have loved you.'

John 15:9-12

Additional scripture readings are listed on page 398.

5 Sermon

6 Hymn

THE BLESSING OF THE MARRIAGE

7 All stand. The minister says:

> Gracious God,
> you have brought *A* and *C* together in love and trust.
>
> By the power of your Holy Spirit,
> may they receive your blessing upon their marriage;
> through Jesus Christ our Lord. **Amen.**

8 The minister says to the husband:

> *A*, you have come here as *C*'s husband
> seeking God's blessing upon your marriage,
> and desiring to live according to God's will.
>
> I ask you, therefore:
> will you love her, comfort and honour her,
> be her companion
> through all the joys and sorrows of life,
> and be faithful to her
> as long as you both shall live?

The husband answers:

> With God's help, I will.

The minister says to the wife:

> *C*, you have come here as *A*'s wife
> seeking God's blessing upon your marriage,
> and desiring to live according to God's will.
>
> I ask you, therefore:
> will you love him, comfort and honour him,
> be his companion
> through all the joys and sorrows of life,
> and be faithful to him
> as long as you both shall live?

The wife answers:

> With God's help, I will.

9 The husband and wife join their ring hands. The minister
places a hand on their joined hands, and says:

> Eternal God,
> bless *these rings/this ring,*
> *symbols/a symbol* of the love and trust
> between *A* and *C*. **Amen.**

10 The minister may wrap her/his stole around their joined
hands. The husband and wife say together:

> Within the love of God,
> Father, Son, and Holy Spirit,
> I am bound to you in marriage
> for better, for worse,
> for richer, for poorer,
> in sickness and in health,
> to love and to cherish,
> until we are parted by death.

11 The people remain standing. The husband and wife may
kneel, and the minister may lay hands upon their heads.

The minister says:

> *A* and *C,*
> the blessing of God the Father,
> God the Son, and God the Holy Spirit,
> be upon you and remain with you always.
> May God be your protection and your wisdom,
> your guide and your peace,
> your joy, your comfort, and your eternal rest. **Amen.**

12 Hymn

13 The whole of the Ministry of the Word follows, if it has not
occurred earlier. If the sermon has been deferred, it is
preached here.

THE PRAYERS

14 All sit.

These or some other prayers of intercession:

Let us pray.

God of grace, source of all love,
we pray for *A* and *C*
that they may live together in love and faithfulness
to the end of their lives.

Lord of life,
hear us in your love.

Enrich their friendship,
that each may be for the other
a companion in joy and a comforter in sorrow.

Lord of life,
hear us in your love.

Help *A* and *C* to be patient, gentle, and forgiving,
that their marriage may reflect Christ's love for all people.

Lord of life,
hear us in your love.

Enable them to make their home
a place of welcome and friendship,
that their life together
may be a source of strength to others.

Lord of life,
hear us in your love.

Other intercessions may be included.

May we, who have witnessed their promises today,
be signs of your love in the world;
through Jesus Christ our Lord. **Amen.**

15 The Lord's Prayer

EITHER

OR

We say together the prayer
that Jesus gave us:

As our Saviour taught his
disciples, we pray:

Our Father in heaven,
hallowed be your Name,
your kingdom come,
your will be done,
on earth as in heaven.
Give us today our daily
    bread.
Forgive us our sins
as we forgive those who
    sin against us.
Save us from the time of
    trial
and deliver us from evil.
For the kingdom, the
    power and the glory
    are yours,
now and for ever. Amen.

Our Father, who art in
    heaven,
hallowed be thy Name;
thy kingdom come;
thy will be done;
on earth as it is in heaven.
Give us this day our
    daily bread.
And forgive us our
    trespasses,
as we forgive those who
    trespass against us.
And lead us not into
    temptation;
but deliver us from evil.
For thine is the kingdom,
    the power, and the
    glory,
for ever and ever. Amen.

16 If Holy Communion is to be celebrated, the service continues
from no. 20.

If Holy Communion is not celebrated, the service continues
as follows:

17 All stand.

The minister says this prayer, or gives thanks in her/his own
words:

Praise God,
who is the source of joy and celebration,
pleasure and delight, love and friendship.

Praise God,
who, in the life and victory of Jesus Christ,
reveals to us the glory of self-giving love.

Praise God,
who sends the Holy Spirit to be our helper
and to guide us into the way of perfect love.

Praise God, Father, Son, and Holy Spirit. Amen.

18 Hymn

19 The minister says to all present:

God the Father, God the Son,
and God the Holy Spirit,
make *you/us* strong in faith
and guide *you/us* in truth and love.

EITHER

OR

The Lord bless you
   and keep you;
the Lord make his face to
   shine on you
and be gracious to you;
the Lord look on you with
   kindness
and give you peace. **Amen.**

May God be gracious to us
   and bless us,
and make his face to shine
upon us. **Amen.**

HOLY COMMUNION

20 The Peace

All stand.

The peace of the Lord be always with you.
And also with you.

The people may greet one another in the name of Christ.

THE PREPARATION OF THE GIFTS

21 Bread and wine are brought to the table by the husband and wife or other members of the congregation (or if already on the table are uncovered). The presiding minister takes the bread and wine and prepares them for use.

THE THANKSGIVING

22 All stand.

The presiding minister leads the great prayer of thanksgiving:

The Lord be with you.
And also with you.

Lift up your hearts.
We lift them to the Lord.

Let us give thanks to the Lord our God.
It is right to give our thanks and praise.

We praise you, gracious God,
creator and sustainer of all things.

From the beginning
you made man and woman
for yourself and for each other,
and you call us to reflect your faithfulness
in lives of love and service.

You gave yourself to us in your Son, Jesus Christ,
the Lord of heaven and earth,
and entrusted him to the care of a human family.
In his life, death and resurrection,
you revealed the power of self-giving love,
rescued us from sin and selfishness
and made us a new family through your grace.

You give yourself to us today,
and by your Holy Spirit
you promise to be with us always
as our companion and our guide.

And so with all your people on earth and in heaven
we give you thanks and praise:

Holy, holy, holy Lord,
God of power and might,
heaven and earth are full of your glory.
Hosanna in the highest.
Blessèd is he who comes in the name of the Lord.
Hosanna in the highest.

Holy God, we praise you
that on the night in which he was betrayed
our Saviour Christ took bread
and gave you thanks.
He broke it, and gave it to his disciples, saying,
'Take, eat. This is my body, given for you.
Do this in remembrance of me.'

After supper, he took the cup of wine,
gave thanks, and gave it to them, saying,
'Drink this, all of you.
This is my blood of the new covenant,
poured out for all people for the forgiveness of sins.
Do this in remembrance of me.'

And so, gracious God, we remember and celebrate
all that Christ has done for us.
We offer ourselves to you in humble thanksgiving.

Send your Holy Spirit
that these gifts of bread and wine
may be for us the body and blood of Christ.
Together with all your people,
may we have life in all its fullness,
live in the power of love,
and fill creation with a song of endless praise.

Through Christ, with Christ, and in Christ,
in the unity of the Holy Spirit,
all glory is yours, God most holy,
now and for ever. Amen.

THE BREAKING OF THE BREAD

23 The presiding minister breaks the bread in the sight of the people in silence, or saying:

The bread we break is a sharing in the body of Christ.

The presiding minister may lift the cup in silence, or saying:

The cup we bless is a sharing in the blood of Christ.

24 Silence, all seated or kneeling

THE SHARING OF THE BREAD AND WINE

25 The presiding minister receives, then, beginning with the husband and wife and their families, the people, according to local custom.

26 Words such as the following are said during the distribution:

The body of Christ. Amen.

The blood of Christ. Amen.

27 During the distribution there may be appropriate music.

28 The elements that remain are covered with a white cloth.

PRAYERS AND DISMISSAL

29 Let us pray.

We thank you, Lord,
that you have fed us in this sacrament,
united us with Christ,
and given us a foretaste of the heavenly banquet
prepared for all people. Amen.

30 Hymn

31 The presiding minister says to all present:

God the Father, God the Son,
and God the Holy Spirit,
make *you/us* strong in faith
and guide *you/us* in truth and love.

EITHER

OR

The Lord bless you
    and keep you;
the Lord make his face to
    shine on you
and be gracious to you;
the Lord look on you with
    kindness
and give you peace. **Amen.**

May God be gracious to us
    and bless us,
and make his face to shine
    upon us. **Amen.**

ADDITIONAL SCRIPTURE READINGS

Old Testament

Genesis 1:26-29*a*, 31*a*	Man and woman created in God's image
Genesis 2:4-9, 15-24	A husband and wife become one flesh
Song of Solomon 1:15 - 2:4	A love song
Isaiah 61:10; 62:3-5	Wedded to God

Psalms

Psalm 23	The Lord our shepherd
Psalm 121	The Lord's protection and blessing
Psalm 127 *or* 128	The gift of a family

Epistle

Romans 12:1-2, 9-13	Love in practice
Ephesians 5:21-31	Husband and wife in Christian marriage
Philippians 1:9-11	Growing into a rich love
Philippians 2:1-11	The example of Jesus
1 John 3:18-24	Love in practice
1 John 4:7-12, 15-17	Love one another
Revelation 19:6-9	The wedding feast of the Lamb of God

Gospel

Matthew 5:1-10	The Beatitudes
Matthew 7:21, 24-27	Hearing and doing
Matthew 22:35-40	The greatest commandment
John 2:1-11	Jesus at a wedding

ACKNOWLEDGEMENTS

Every effort has been made to ensure that the following list of acknowledgements is as comprehensive as possible, but the experience of those involved in the preparation of **The Methodist Worship Book** is similar to that of the compilers of the **Book of Common Order** of the Church of Scotland, who state:

> Many sources have contributed to the compilation of this book, and not all of them are now traceable. Individual members of the Committee prepared drafts, which were revised more or less drastically by the Committee, often resulting in final versions which looked little like the original drafts. Among the casualties of this sometimes protracted process was the identity of many of the sources; they could not be recalled, nor did there seem to be any way to track them down. The Panel wishes to record at once both its indebtedness to any who may recognise in this book rhythms and patterns, expressions and phrases, ideas and images which are their own, and its regret that it became impossible to ask permission or seek consent for their inclusion . . .

> If, through inadvertence, copyright material has been used without permission or acknowledgement, the publisher will be grateful to be informed and will be pleased to make the necessary correction in subsequent editions.

The symbol * in the following paragraphs denotes that a text has been altered.

Except where indicated below, all psalms, scripture readings and scripture sentences are taken from **The New Revised Standard Version of the Bible (Anglicized Edition)**, © 1989, 1995 by the Division of Christian Education of the National Council of Churches of Christ in the United States of America, and are used by permission. All rights reserved.

Some scripture sentences are from **The Revised Standard Version**, © 1946 and 1952 by the Division of Christian Education of the National Council of Churches of Christ in the United States of America, and are used by permission. All rights reserved.

Some scripture sentences are from **The Revised English Bible**, © 1989 Oxford University Press and Cambridge University Press.

One scripture sentence comes from **The New Jerusalem Bible**, © 1985 Darton Longman & Todd and Doubleday & Co. Inc.